I0397202

DEFINE THAT SYSTEM

ISBN: 978-1-291-15094-0

Copyright   ©   Andreas Sofroniou 2012

Copyright   ©   Andreas Sofroniou 2012

DEFINE THAT SYSTEM

ISBN: 978-1-291-15094-0

CONTENTS:

1 MANAGEMENT OF INFORMATION SYSTEMS   6
2 IMPORTANCE OF MODELS AND METHODS   8
3 ADMINISTRATION AND INFORMATION SYSTEMS   9
4 PROJECT MANAGEMENT AND PLANNING 12
5 COST AND BENEFITS ANALYSIS   13
6 MANAGING PROJECTS   15
6.1 DEFINITION 15
6.2 PROBLEMS   15
6.3 SOLUTIONS 16
6.4 PROJECT BOARD 17
6.5 PROJECT MANAGER   18
6.6 STAGE MANAGER 19
6.7 PLANNING   19
6.8 PRODUCT BREAKDOWN STRUCTURES   20
6.9 PRODUCT FLOW DIAGRAM   20
6.10 MANAGEMENT QUALITY   20
6.11 PROJECT INITIATION   21
6.12 REVIEWS   21
6.13 ASSESSMENT   22
6.14 PROJECT CLOSURE   22
6.15 CHECKPOINT MEETING   23
6.16 QUALITY REVIEW   23
7   BUSINESS SYSTEM DEVELOPMENT 24
7.1 PROCEDURES DIAGRAMS   29
7.2 PURPOSE   30
7.3 HIERARCHICAL DIAGRAM OF BUSINESS SYSTEM DEVELOPMENT   31
7.4 UNDERSTANDING THE PROCEDURES OF THE PROJECTS DEVELOPMENT 32
8 PROJECT FRAMEWORK   34

1 MANAGEMENT OF INFORMATION SYSTEMS

The most important functions that top executives perform include setting policies, planning, and preparing budgets. At the strategic level, these decision-making functions are supported by executive information systems. The objective of these systems is to gather, analyze, and integrate internal (corporate) and external (public) data into dynamic profiles of key corporate indicators.

Depending on the nature of the organization's business, such indicators may relate to the status of high-priority programs, health of the economy, inventory and cash levels, performance of financial markets, relevant efforts of competitors, utilization of manpower, legislative events, and so forth.

The indicators are displayed as text, tables, graphics, or time series, and optional access is provided to more detailed data. The data emanate not only from within the organization's production and administrative departments but also from external information sources, such as public databases.

Present-day efforts, drawing on research in neural computers and networks, are to enhance executive information systems with adaptive and self-organizing abilities by means of learning from the executives' changing information needs and uses.

In military organizations, the approximate equivalent of executive information systems is command-and-control systems. Their purpose is to maintain control over some domain and, if needed, initiate corrective action. Their key characteristic is the real-time nature of the monitoring and decision-making functions.

A command-and-control system typically assumes that the environment exercises pressure on the domain of interest (say, a naval force); the system then monitors the environment (collects intelligence data), analyses the data, compares it with the desired state of the domain, and suggests actions to be taken. Systems of this kind are used at both strategic and tactical levels.

Both executive and military command-and-control systems make use of computational aids for data classification, modeling, and simulation. These capabilities are characteristic of a decision-support system (DSS), a composite of computer techniques for supporting executive decision making in relatively unstructured problem situations.

Decision-support software fails into one of two categories: decision-aid programs, in which the decision maker assigns weighted values to every factor in the decision, and decision-modeling programs, in which the user explores different strategies to arrive at the desired outcome.

2 IMPORTANCE OF MODELS AND METHODS

Because of the enormous complexity of typical production operations and the almost infinite number of changes that can be made and the alternatives that can be pursued, a productive body of quantitative methods has been developed to solve production management problems.

Most of these techniques have emerged from the fields of industrial engineering, operations research, and systems engineering. Specialists in these fields are increasingly using computers and information processing to solve production problems involving the masses of data associated with large numbers of workers, massive inventories, and huge quantities of work in process that characterize most of today's production operations. Indeed, many mass production operations could not run without the support of these industrial engineers and technical specialists.

3 ADMINISTRATION AND INFORMATION SYSTEMS

Administrative functions in formal organizations have as their objective the husbanding and optimization of corporate resources--namely, employees and their activities, inventories of materials and equipment, facilities, and finances.

Administrative information systems support this objective. Commonly called management information systems (MIS), they focus primarily on resource administration and provide top management with reports of aggregate data. Executive information systems may be viewed as an evolution of administrative information systems in the direction of strategic tracking, modeling, and decision making.

Typically, administrative information systems consist of a number of modules, each supporting a particular function. The modules share a common database whose contents may, however, be distributed over a number of machines and locations, Financial information systems have evolved from the initial applications of punched cards before World War II to integrated accounting and finance systems that cover general accounting, accounts receivable and payable, payroll, purchasing, inventory control, and financial statements such as balance sheets.

Functionally close to payroll systems are personnel information systems, which support the administration of the organization's human resources. Job and salary histories, inventory of skills, performance reviews, and other types of personnel data are combined in the database to assist personnel administration, explore potential effects of reorganization or new salary scales (or changes in benefits), and match job requirements with skills.

Project management information systems concentrate on resource allocation and task completion of organized activities; they usually incorporate such scheduling methods as the critical path method (CPM) or program evaluation and review technique (PERT).

Since the advent of laptops and all other designs of microcomputers, information processing in organizations has become heavily supported by office automation tools. These involve six basic applications: text processing, database, spreadsheet, graphics, communications, and networking.

Administrative systems in smaller organizations are usually built as extensions of office automation tools; in large organizations these tools form an interface to custom software. The current trend in office automation is toward integrating the first five applications into a software utility, either delivered to each microprocessor workstation from a "server" on the corporate computer network or integrated into other applications software.

Administrative information systems abound in organizations in both the private and public sectors throughout the industrialized world. In the retail industry, point-of-sale terminals are linked into distributed administrative information systems that contain financial and inventory modules at the department, store, geographic area, and corporate chain levels, with modeling facilities that help to determine marketing strategies and optimize profits.

Administrative information systems are indispensable to government; the agencies of virtually all U.S. municipalities with more than 10,000 inhabitants use such systems. The systems are generally centered on a generic database management system and are increasingly supported by software modules and programs that permit data modeling, i.e. they acquire management orientation.

4 PROJECT MANAGEMENT AND PLANNING

Project managers frequently face the task of controlling projects that contain unknown and unpredictable factors. When the projects are not complex, bar charts can be used to plan and control project activities. These charts divide the project into discrete activities or tasks and analyze each task individually to indicate weekly manpower requirements. As the work goes forward, progress is charted and estimates are made on the effects of any delays or difficulties encountered during the

Many variations and extensions of the two original techniques are now in use, and they have proved particularly valuable for projects requiring the co-coordinated work of hundreds of separate contractors. The use of project planning and control techniques now common in all types of civil engineering and construction work, as well as for large developmental projects such as the manufacture of aircraft, missiles, space vehicles, and large mainframe computer systems.

5 COST AND BENEFITS ANALYSIS

In the areas in which technology advances fastest, new products and new materials are required in a constant flow, but there are many industries in which the rate of change is gentle. Although ships, automobiles, telephones, and television receivers have changed over the last quarter of a century, the changes have not been spectacular. Nevertheless, a manufacturer who used methods even 10 years old could not survive in these businesses.

These efforts to improve existing products and processes have been formalized under the titles of value engineering and cost-benefit analysis.

In value engineering every complete product and every component have their primary function described by an action verb and a noun. For example, an automobile's dynamo, or generator, generates electricity. The engineer considers all other possible methods of generation, calculates a cost for each, and compares the lowest figure with that for the existing dynamo.

If the ratio is reasonably close to unity, the dynamo can be accepted as an efficient component. If not, the engineer examines the alternatives in more detail. The same treatment is applied in turn to each of the parts out of which the chosen component is built, until it is clear that the best possible value is being obtained.

Cost-benefit analysis approaches the same fundamental problem from a different angle. It takes each part of a product or process and completely defines its function and the basis for measuring its benefits or effectiveness. Then the costs of obtaining each part are reviewed, taking full account of purchased material, labor, investment cost, downtime, and other factors.

This focuses attention upon the most expensive items and makes it possible to apply the principal effort in seeking economies at the points of maximum reward. In the effort to improve a product or process, care must be taken to evaluate alternatives on the same 'cost" and "benefit" bases so that existing approaches do not enjoy a special advantage just because they are familiar.

These two processes are unending. Every new material, new manufacturing technique, or new way of carrying out an operation gives the engineer a chance to improve his product, and it is from these continuing improvements that the high degree of economy and reliability of modern equipment derives.

6 MANAGING PROJECTS

6.1 DEFINITION

Business organizations often have problems in deciding and it is very easy to take a narrow view. For example, many people believe that a project must involve computers in some way. However, a much broader view is required when the following definition is considered.

"A project is a management environment, set up to deliver a business product to a specified business case".

In other words, a project is temporary, with a temporary organization which only exists to deliver something (a product) which is considered worthwhile to the business. This temporary situation has two important characteristics. It is a one-off and it is introducing change via the delivered products.

Project products are wide ranging and diverse in their scope. The resulting product may be a bridge, a road, the procurement of equipment, restructuring an organization, relocating an office, or a computer system. The environment created and the work done to deliver the product is a project.

6.2 PROBLEMS

Projects are conceived and grow from a business need, but what seems clear at the beginning often becomes blurred and confused. In the end projects may not deliver what was expected and costly investment produces few benefits.

It is little wonder that things go wrong and projects fail, not because people are ineffective, but because of the sheer complexity of project management. A recent Butler Cox, UK statistical survey found that 80% of the reasons for project failure were management, not technical.

Some of the problems which may be familiar to management at all levels are:

- No standard approach to project management
- Lack of communication
- Inadequate planning
- Inadequate controls
- Inadequate Business Case to justify the project
- Unclear project definition, and objectives
- Uncontrolled change
- Skills shortage of experienced people
- Inadequate team building and staff motivation
- Taking uncontrolled shortcuts
- Inadequate documentation
- Lack of commitment
- Inadequate quality standards.

6.3 SOLUTIONS

Unlike line management, which deals with operational issues and maintaining existing services, project management deals with the unprecedented, the unfamiliar and the need for change.

Over the years it has become recognized that there is a common thread running through the management of projects. Much of this is common sense and it was the formalization of this common sense, plus traditional management good practice, into a structure which gave rise to project management methods.

There are many project management methods available, each of which is characterized by the way in which it provides principles, procedures and techniques for the management of projects. Methods utilize existing standard techniques as well as introducing their own unique features.

It is probably impossible for all projects to succeed, but the number of project failures can be dramatically reduced by the proper application of a structured project management method.

6.4 PROJECT BOARD

- Within the constraints imposed by the IT Executive Committee (ITEC), the Project Board:
- Has authority for the project
- Appoints the Project Manager, Stage Manager(s) and Project Assurance Team
- Defines their responsibilities and objectives
- Approves Project and Stage level plans and commits resources
- Gives direction and guidance
- Sets tolerances
- Approves the Project Initiation Document
- Conducts Mid Stage and End Stage Assessments

- Approves Exception Plans
- Reports status to ITEC
- Authorizes the start of each stage
- Authorizes project closure
- May recommend project termination

6.5 PROJECT MANAGER

- Defines responsibilities within the project
- Prepares Project and Stage level plans
- Sets objectives and responsibilities for the stage managers
- Schedules Stage control points
- Creates a Configuration Management Structure
- Prepares periodic Highlight Reports
- Presents Stage status at Mid Stage and End Stage Assessment meetings (MSA and ESA)
- Enforces Technical Exception procedures
- Prepares Exception Plans
- Arranges Walkthroughs
- Increases possibilities for the success of the project

6.6 STAGE MANAGER

- Defines objectives and responsibilities for stage teams
- Prepares any necessary detailed plans

- Monitors progress and costs of stage teams, and initiates any necessary corrective action
- Ensures that Technical Exceptions are properly reported, evaluated, and initiates appropriate actions
- Liaises with the Project Assurance Team to ensure the integrity of the stage
- Maintains the Stage File
- Ensures that Quality Reviews are held as planned.

6.7 PLANNING

The start of the planning process is to identify the products needed, by means of a Product Breakdown Structure.

An explicit Product Description, including quality criteria, is prepared and agreed for each product to confirm the requirement.

Identifying the derivation of each product from previous products and the quality review process required helps produce an activity network and points to the resources needed and the timescales.

6.8 PRODUCT BREAKDOWN STRUCTURES

A Project Management product breakdown structure is a hierarchy of products required to complete a given project. At each level in the hierarchy, products are the total components of the level above.

A Project Management method provides a generic model product breakdown structure for an IT system down to the third level, which gives a starting point for project-specific planning

Use of the model helps ensure a complete project definition from the outset. Any product not required is struck through. Products which are required, but which will not be provided by the project (because they already exist, or will be provided by another project), are suitably annotated. In this way, all can see what is, and what is not, included within the scope of the project.

6.9 PRODUCT FLOW DIAGRAM

The Product Breakdown Structure shows only product content. The Product Flow Diagram is prepared to show product dependencies – i.e., the logical sequence in which products need to be developed. This enables the planner to complete product descriptions, identify gaps in the product set, and subsequently develop the activity network.

6.10 MANAGEMENT QUALITY

The management products of a project are those documents which facilitate effective management of that project. They are produced *as a* result of organising, planning and controlling the project and include job descriptions, plans, Checkpoint meeting reports ant highlight reports (filed in the appropriate stage file). They do not form part of the final system.

The quality products are those products which establish the required quality of the project's products, and the actions needed to check that the products are of the required quality. Examples are product descriptions (which include quality criteria and the method of review), invitations to quality reviews, Project Issue Reports, etc. They are filed in the Quality File.

6.11 PROJECT INITIATION

- Project Board control points:
- Formally initiate the project
- Agree the objectives
- Confirm the responsibilities
- Review the Project Plans and first Stage Plans
- Review the business and security risks and ensure that proposals to meet them are adequate
- Review and agree the Project Initiation Document.

6.12 REVIEWS

- Project Board mandatory control points
- Review actual completion of stage against plans
- Identify problems, existing and potential
- Review project status against plans
- Assure technical and business integrity
- Review business and security risks
- Compare next stage plans with Project Resource Plan/ Project Technical Plan
- Approve progress to next stage
- Report to ITEC

6.13 ASSESSMENT

- Planned, for long stages
- as confidence boost for management
- to allow commencement of the next overlapping stage
- . Unplanned, to review
- serious technical exception
- Exception Plan.

6.14 PROJECT CLOSURE

- Ensure that all information to run the system is documented
- Conduct the Project Evaluation Review
- Arrange the Post Implementation Review
- Authorize formal closure of the project
- Report to participants.

6.15 CHECKPOINT MEETING

- Record progress on technical activities
- Record status of stage products
- Record actual resource usage
- Identify technical problems
- Signal the need for an Exception Plan
- Prepare Checkpoint report for Project Manager.

6.16 QUALITY REVIEW

- To ensure product quality (completion, compliance with requirements, quality, use of standards)
- To discover and document errors
- Specify defined Quality Review responsibilities
- Special forms and checklists
- Covers the follow up options and procedures.

8 BUSINESS SYSTEM DEVELOPMENT

DIAGRAMMATIC REPRESENTATIONS

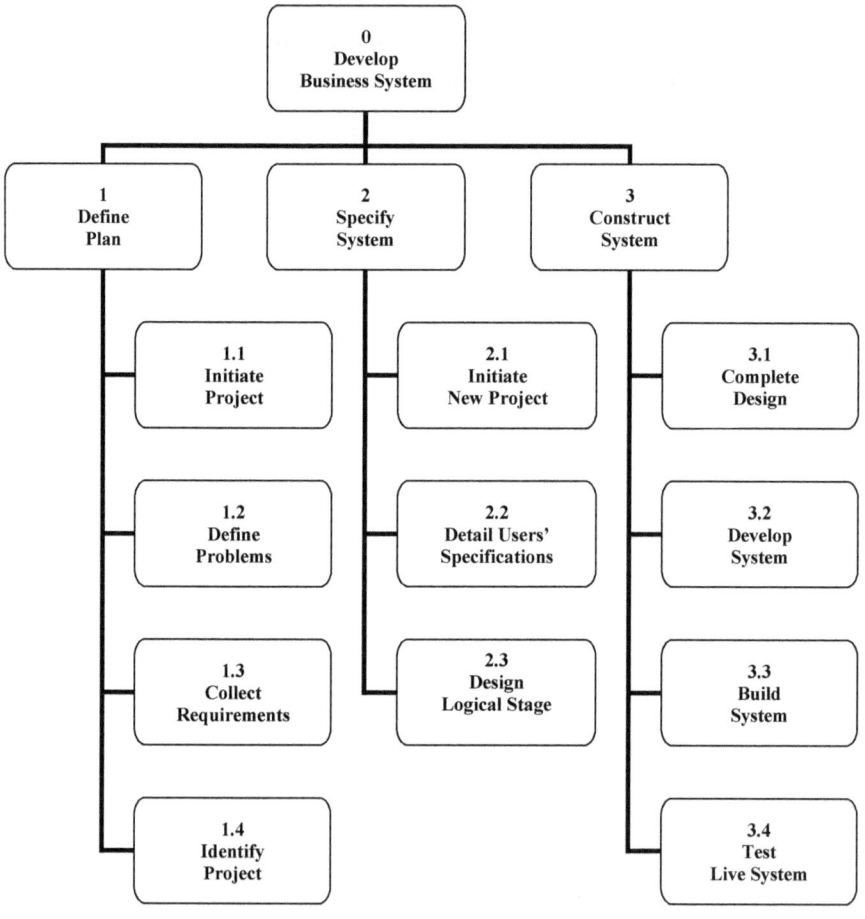

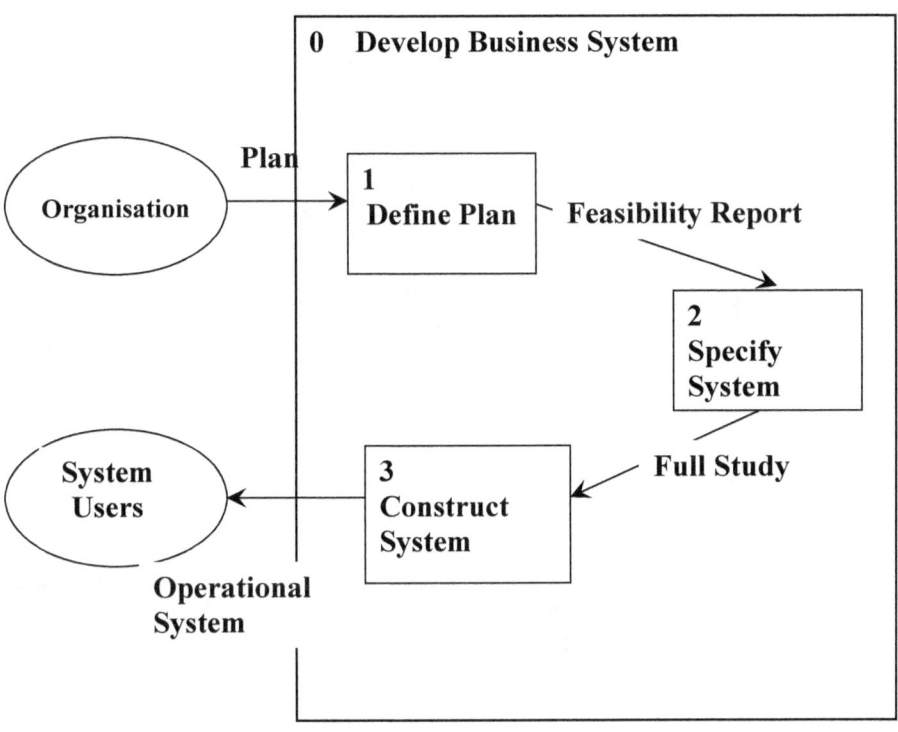

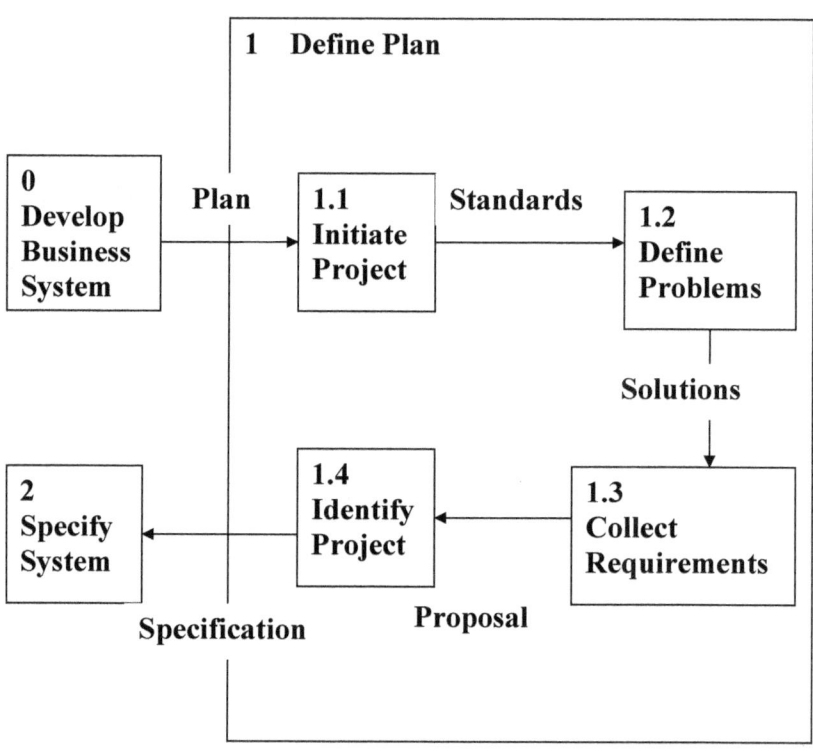

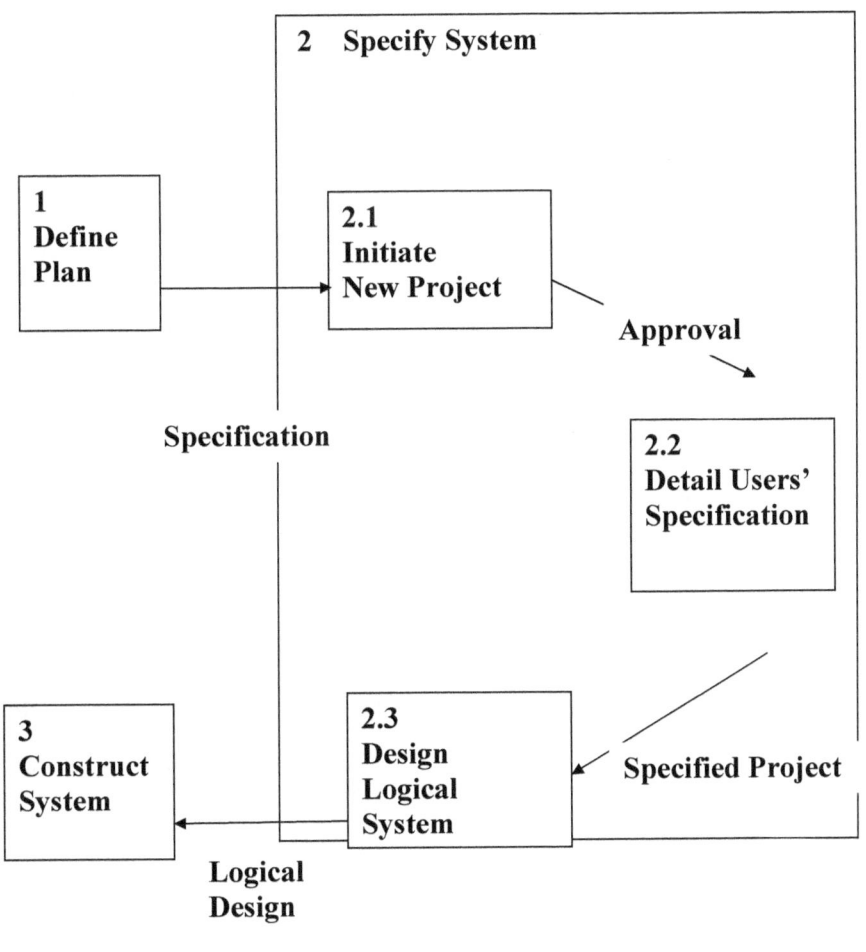

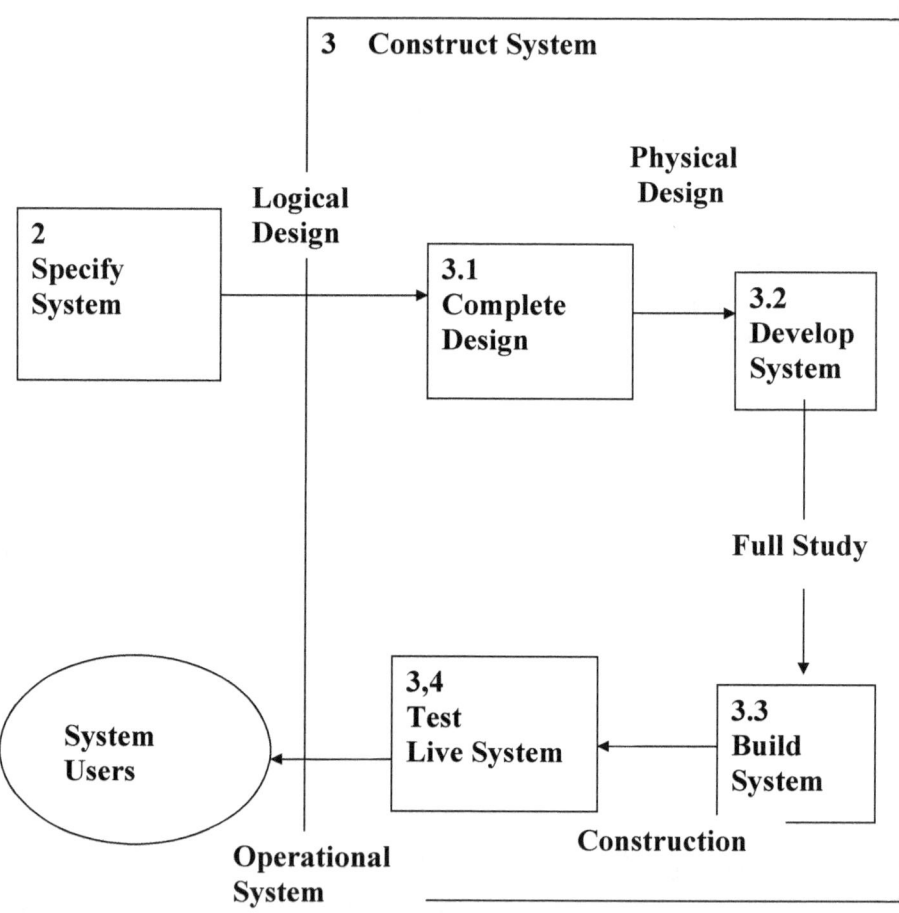

7.1 PROCEDURES DIAGRAMMATIC REPRESENTATION

Typical Stages of Development

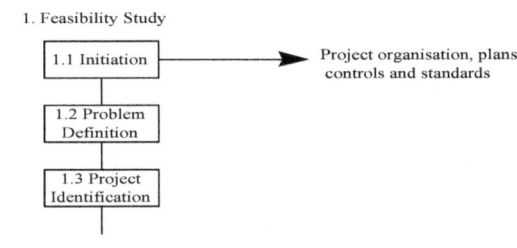

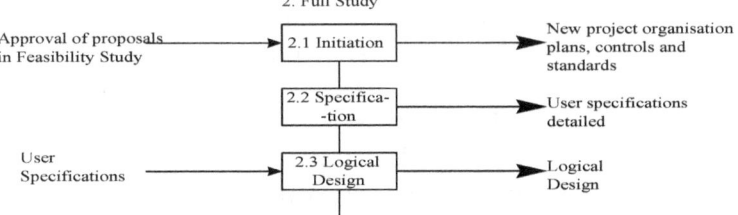

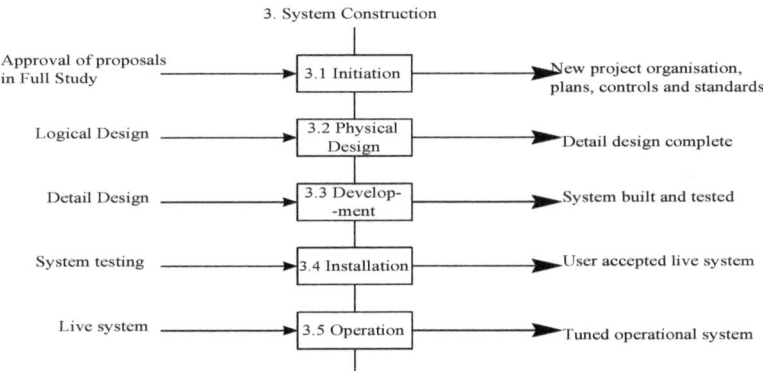

7.2 PURPOSE

This section of the book is intended to give Project Management staff an overview of the Project Development Methods and some indication of how these relate to the various Project Management Techniques. It should also he useful to Analysts, Designers and Programmers as an introduction to the more detailed understanding they will require of the methods. It is not a definitive statement of any established Project Management Procedures, Techniques or Documentation, but rather a quick reference guide. It will, from time to time, be out of line with detailed manuals to which reference should be made when necessary.

7.3 HIERARCHICAL DIAGRAM OF BUSINESS SYSTEM DEVELOPMENT

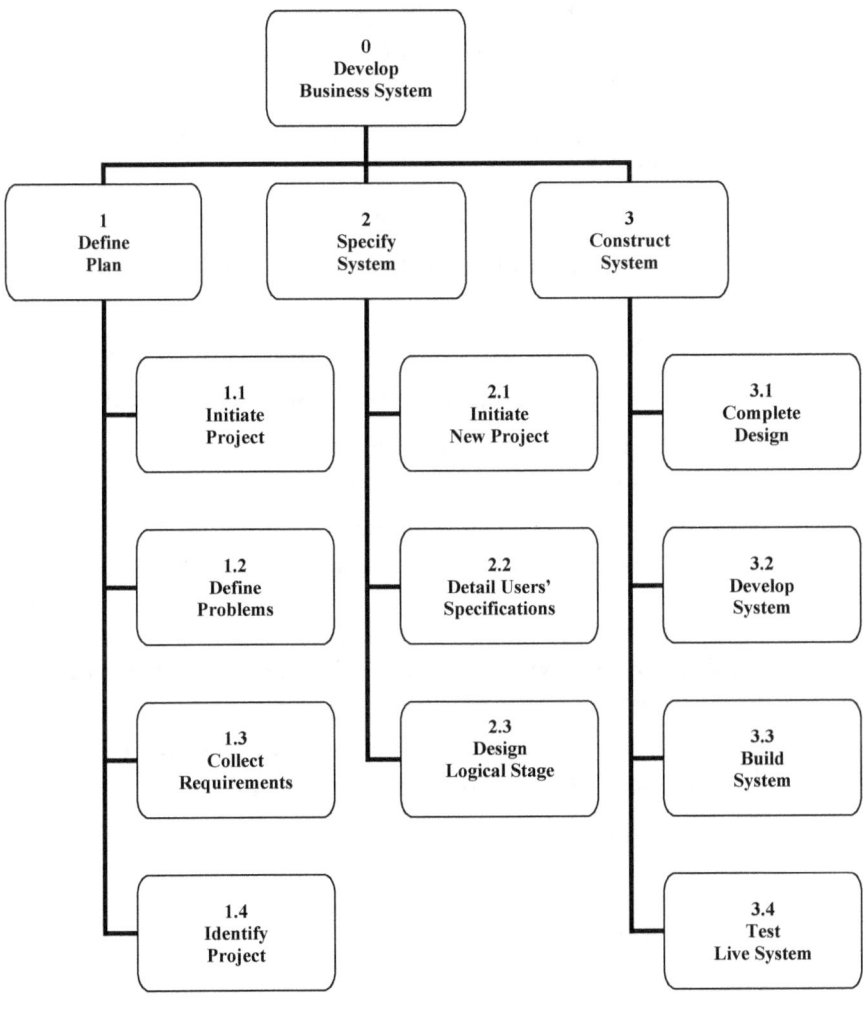

7.4 UNDERSTANDING THE PROCEDURES OF THE PROJECTS DEVELOPMENT.

A system is a set of procedures (manual & computer) for carrying out some Business Tasks such as Purchase Bought-out Parts, Control Stock, Invoice Customers, Develop System (PM & DM is a system for developing systems!).

Whereas a project is a task set up to develop a system.

Projects have the following characteristics:

- Defined End Product, a measurably Improved system
- Defined Timescale, a practical time for the task
- Defined Budget, appropriate to the benefit
- Each one is different; developing systems is not like manufacturing cars.

In this sense 'develop' means change or, better still, improve the system. It is in a different state after the project than before e.g. it may have new computer facilities, it may require a different staff organization. Developing systems can be likened to Improving a property.

When improving a property we must first of all ask why we wish to improve it. Do we want?

- more room,
- more privacy,
- a warmer house.

Having decided why we must tell an architect what we want:

- two more bedrooms,
- a double garage,
- Central heating.

What constraints apply?

- maximum space available,
- budget,
- time.

Having decided what with the architect, he will work out how to implement the solution:

- materials to use,
- strength they should be,
- regulations to be adhered to.

The architect having decided how can now instruct a builder to produce the solution.

The builder having produced a solution will enable us to move in the new rooms, say:

- install the furniture and fittings,
- decorate.

Having moved in we may find there are some changes we wish to make and for some of these we way have to have the builder in. Hopefully the changes won't be of such significance that we have to go back to the architect.

8 PROJECT FRAMEWORK

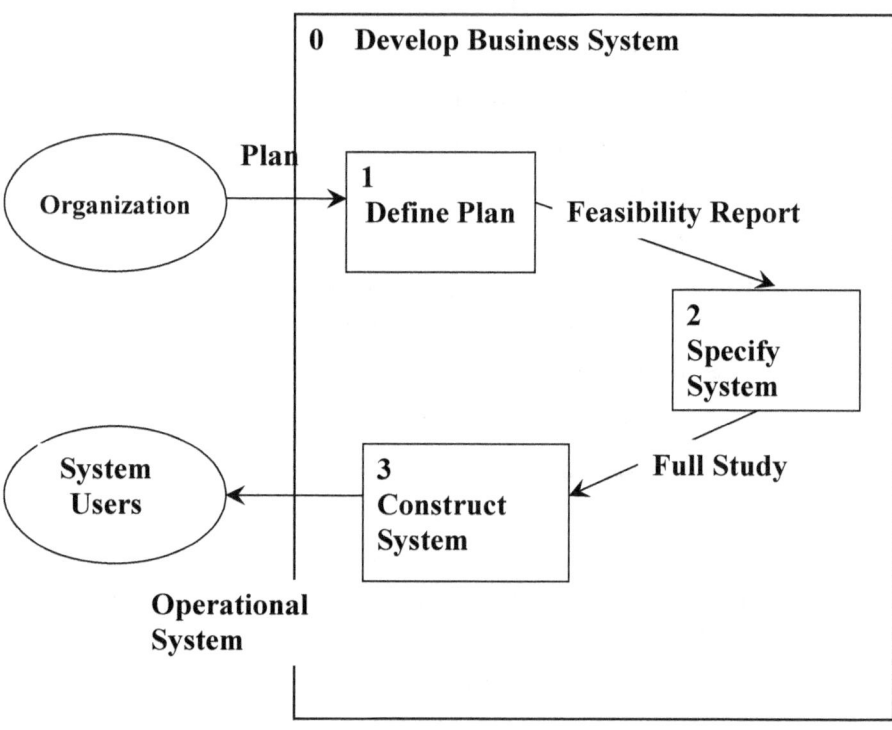

8.1 PURPOSE OF FRAMEWORK

The purpose of the Framework is to define the steps in a Project, which is set up to produce a new operational System. That is, a version of the System which is an Improvement on the previous one.

To achieve this, Projects are broken down into Stages. There are nine Stages, the first and last of which (Initiation and Post Implementation Review) can be regarded as Pre and Post Project activities.

Each stage has a defined set of deliverables.

- Project Initiation,
- Justification,
- Requirement Definition,
- Business Design,
- Technical Design,
- Development,
- Installation,
- Operations Consolidation,
- Post-implementation Review.

8.2 STAGE DELIVERABLES

Generally each Stage delivers a report for management (e.g. a Business Design Report) and a technical document for the next stage (e.g. a Systems Definition).

The Reports are basically updates of the original Justification Report. Thus, each Report is concerned with:

- confirming the business case
- reporting what has happened to date
- Proposing what should happen next.

The contents of the Reports develop as the Project moves on to reflect the decisions relevant to the Stages.

The Technical documents define what has been produced during the current Stage. This, together with documents produced in earlier Stages, enables the next Stage to proceed.

8.3 STRUTCTURE OF DOCUMENTATION

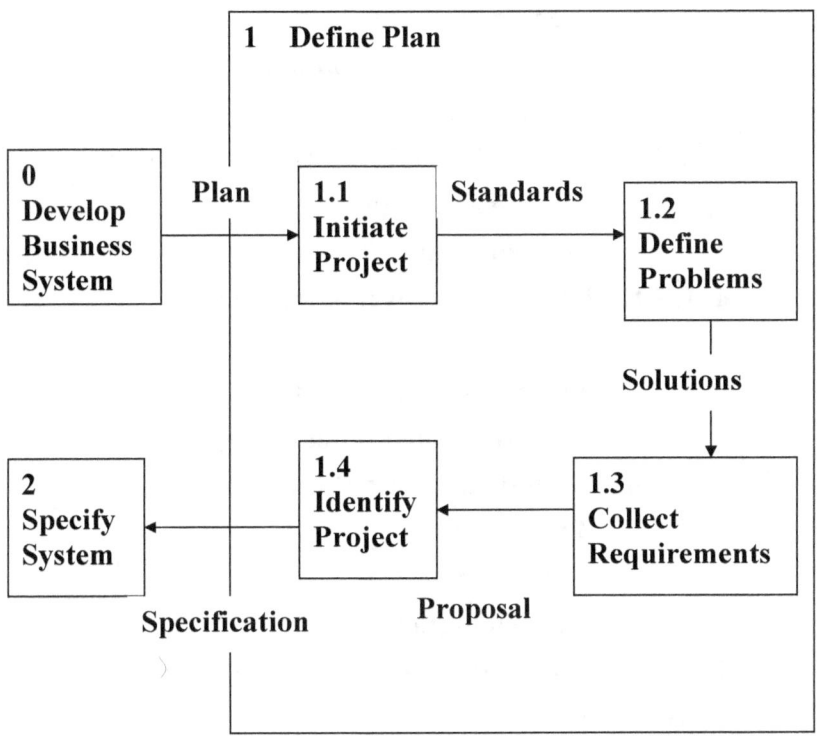

For documentation purposes the Framework is sub-divided into three manuals:

SPECIFICATION covers four Stages:

>Initiation

>Justification

>Requirements Definition

>Business Design

DESIGN AND DEVELOPMENT covers two Stages:

>Technical Design

>Development

IMPLEMENTATION covers three Stages:

>Installation

>Operations Consolidation

>Post Implementation Review

Each manual is divided into three volumes:

>Procedures

>Techniques

>Documentation

8.4 GUIDE TO PROJECT DEVELOPMENT

8.4.1 APPLICABILITY

THE SIMPLIFIED PROCEDURES FOR I.T. PROJECTS DEVELOPMENT can be used on a whole range of Projects from the most complex to the most simple. As mentioned earlier every project is different and experience and judgement are required to apply any project management and development methods.

Some very general guidelines are given below but in practice each Project, large or small, should be looked at in its own right.

These plans will detail:

- Stage Activities required for next Stage
- How these are to be carried out (the detailed tasks).

The tasks for a particular project may be identical to the standard project management and development methods ones or may contain fewer or extra activities according to the needs identified by each proceeding Stage.

8.4.2 OVERLAPPING STAGES

The Framework defines all the Stages and Checkpoints applicable to a development Project. In general the Stages are carried out sequentially i.e. one Stage is completed before the next is commenced.

A Stage Manager, however, may decide that he wishes to start up the next Stage before the current Stage is completed. Any overlapping implies a risk that decisions still to be taken in the current Stage may impact on work done in the next. However, In order to optimize use of resources this may be preferable to waiting until the previous Stage is complete.

An End-Stage assessment of the current stage must still be conducted when the current stage has been completed.

8.4.3 OVERLAPPING STAGE ACTIVITIES

Within a Stage, the Stage Activities, or tasks, are in general sequential i.e. one task is completed before the next is commenced. There is more scope here for overlapping tasks, but again there is a danger of additional iteration between tasks resulting in more total work. The decision to overlap tasks within a stage is the responsibility of the Stage Manager.

8.4.4 REPORTING POINTS

On smaller projects it may be desirable to reduce the reporting overhead by combining stages together and treating them as a single stage for prompt and reporting purposes.

Every project, however small, must report at the Justification Stage. The reason for this is that, included In the Justification Stage are the tasks for justifying the Project Leader. i.e. establishing the business case, identifying which Stages, tasks and Checkpoints the Project will observe, and preparing plans and budgets for the Project.

Broadly speaking, for reporting purposes, the following rules can be applied:

Simple Projects - Report after Justification, Development and Implementation

Moderate Projects - Report after Justification, Technical Design, Development and Implementation

Complex Projects - Reports after every Stage. Though for smaller ones Requirements Definition & Business Design may be combined.

8.5 RELATIONSHIP TO PROJECT MANAGEMENT AND DEVELOPMENT METHODS

8.5.1 PLANNING

THE SIMPLIFIED PROCEDURES FOR I.T. PROJECTS DEVELOPMENT prescribes basically two types of Plans - Business (concerned with resources) and Technical (concerned with activities & timescales).

For each type of plan there are three levels of detail. These correspond to THE SIMPLIFIED PROCEDURES FOR I.T. PROJECTS DEVELOPMENT levels of stage, stage activities and detailed procedures. The Stages are planned at the beginning for the whole Project (see Justification). Stage Activities and Detailed Procedures are planned Stage by Stage.

8.5.2 CONTROL

Stage Activities and Detailed Procedures also form the framework for Control.

The corresponding controls are called:

- End Stage Assessments
- Milestones
- Inspections

These form a hierarchy.

Inspections are the lowest level controls, the basic building blocks and are conducted strictly to, what are called, STRUCTURED WALKTHROUGH standards.

Typically subjects for Inspections are:

- Context Diagrams
- Individual Activity Diagrams and associated definitions

- **Activity Diagram Sets**
- **Data Model Components**
- **Program Modules**
- **Programs.**

The subjects of Inspections are the Individual Items in the Checklists for Milestones THE SIMPLIFIED PROCEDURES FOR I.T. PROJECTS DEVELOPMENT manual. The timing of them will be determined by those carrying out the detailed procedures.

Milestones are concerned with checking that all the required Inspections took place by the right people, at the right time, on the right product. They generally occur at the end of a Stage Activity (such as "Examine Existing System").

End Stage Assessments are concerned with the completeness and quality of stage. The deliverables are built up section by section from the work done during Stage Activities, Completeness and Quality Checks.

9 DOCUMENT RESULTS.

The results of Inspections and Milestones should be documented on a WALKTHROUGH CONTROL NOTE PROCEDURES OVERVIEW.

9.1 PROJECT INITIATION STAGE

Outline:

> 'Control Change' Is the mechanism for initiating Projects This 'Initiation' Stage will enable the project to start by carrying out certain outstanding tasks, which should have been done in Change Control.

Objectives:

- Establish Terms of Reference for a Justification Stage, within the objectives and constraints determined by a Business Activity or other study,

- Establish resource requirements, expected timescale and cost of the Justification Stage,

- Set up the Project organization for the Justification Stage as appropriate.

9.2 JUSTIFICATION STAGE

Outline:

> The Justification Stage examines the potential application area(s) identified by management. The scope of the Justification Stage will be constrained by the Terms of Reference, which will reflect any prior study.

> The Justification Stage generally adopts a broad-brush approach, involving some analysis

and some outline design. The purpose is to commit a limited expenditure in order to establish whether it is worth conducting a detailed Investigation.

Objectives:

- Define the Scope,
- Outline the requirements,
- Identify possible solutions and select with the users the most appropriate,
- Establish technical and operational feasibility,
- Demonstrate financial and business justification and Identify other benefits,
- Identify relevant Stages for the Project, and prepare detailed estimates for the next Stage and provisional estimates for all subsequent Stages,
- Plan implementation and educational strategy,
- Produce a Justification Report to enable management to determine whether to continue to the next Stage.

9.3 JUSTIFICATION

THE STAGES:

- Determine Scope And Plan Study
- Examine Existing System
- Determine Requirements

- Evaluate Solutions
- Prepare Implementation and Develop Plans
- Draft And Review Justification Report
- Seek Approval.

9.4 PROJECT BOARD RESPONSIBILITIES

Within the constraints imposed by the Executive Committee, the Project Board:

- Has authority for the project,
- Appoints the Project and Stage Managers, and defines their responsibilities and objectives,
- Approves project and stage level plans and commits resources,
- Gives direction and guidance,
- Approves the Project Initiation Document,
- Conducts Mid stage and end stage Assessments,
- Approves exception plans
- Reports status to Executive Committee,
- Authorizes the start of each stage,
- Authorizes project closure,
- May recommend project termination.

10 REQUIREMENTS DEFINITION STAGE

10.1 DEFINITION

Outline:

The Requirement Definition Stage follows acceptance of the Justification Report by management and authorization from the Project Board to Proceed. During this Stage the application area is analysed more thoroughly, and requirements for the system defined in detail. An outline description of the system in user orientated terms is produced.

Objectives:

- Define in detail the operational & Information requirements for the system,

- Set clear performance targets and acceptance criteria for these requirements,

- Confirm/revise the system proposed by the Justification Stage,

- Produce a design in sufficient detail to confirm the technical approach and identify critical areas of system performance,

- Produce User Requirement Report to enable Management to decide whether the Project should proceed to the Business Design Stage,

- Produce User Requirement Specification as a formal definition of the user's Detailed Requirements.

10.2 REQUIREMENTS DEFINITION STEPS

- **Determine Scope And Objectives**

- **Analyze Existing System**

- **Determine Detailed Requirements**

- **Develop, Outline New System**

- **Update Implementation and Development Plans**

- **Draft Review And Report**

- **Seek Approval**

10.3 REQUIREMENT DEFINITION STAGE ACTIVITIES

- **Familiarize with Justification Report recommendations. Ensure scope has not changed.**

- **Carry out detailed analysis of existing system identifying all basic level activities and data requirements. Produce Activity Diagrams and supporting documentation to required level of detail (2-3 levels from the context diagram usually). Produce High Level Data Model. Identify major problems and costs.**

- **Identify all basic requirements from existing system plus the additional requirements from the KPF analysis and any other requirements needed to overcome the problems. Define measures and targets. Determine which activities need to change, or be included, to meet the specified targets.**

- **Ensure that, in the light of the Detailed Requirements, a possible solution can still be** provided. Produce first level Activity Diagram and documentation to outline the new system.

- Update General Technical Plan and Macro Plan. Produce next Stage Activity Plan and Measurement Plan.
- Collate User Requirement Report, User Requirement Specification
- Seek Project Board Approval.

11 BUSINESS DESIGN STAGE

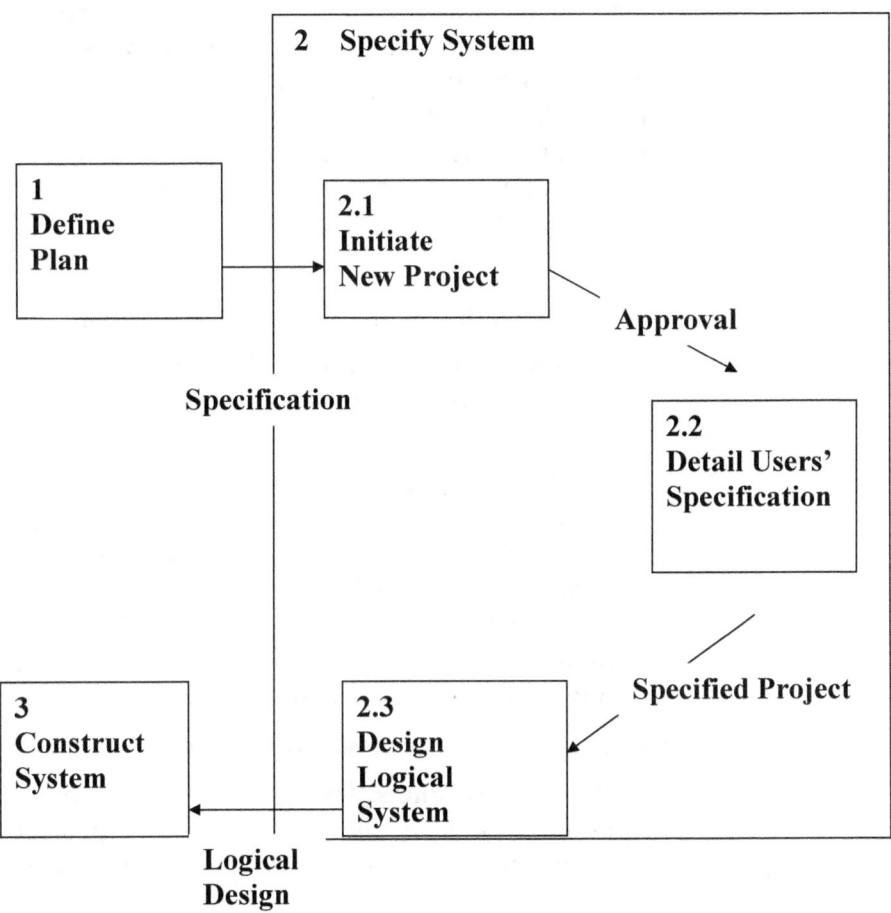

11.1 DEFINITION

Outline:

The Business Design Stage follows acceptance of the User Requirement Report by management and authorization from the Project Board to proceed. During this Stage, the business, or external, design is completed and a detailed specification of the new System In user orientated terms is produced.

Objectives:

- Establish the detail of the business system.

- Validate the Business Design produced and review the technical feasibility of transactions proposed,

- Produce Systems Definition to enable the User to decide whether his Requirements are being satisfied and his Targets being met, to provide a basis of Information for use In the Technical Design Stage. Including the definition of input/output layouts and business processing rules.

- Establish User Acceptance Strategy,

- Produce Business Design Report to enable management to decide whether the project should proceed to the Technical Design Stage.

11.2 BUSINESS DESIGN STEPS

- Business Design Orientation
- Perform Data Analysis

- Develop Detailed System
- Produce User Acceptance Test Strategy
- Update Implementation And Development Plans
- Draft Review System Documents
- Seek Approval.

11.3 BUSINESS DESIGN STAGE ACTIVITIES

- Familiarization with all project documentation produced up to this point.
- Perform Data Analysis to produce a Data Model of the system data.
- Produce a detailed definition of the proposed system.
- Produce Activity Diagrams to 2 or 3 levels of hierarchy with all supporting documentation.
- Produce an Acceptance Test Strategy with the users
- Update General Technical Plan & Macro Plan.
- Produce next Stage Activity Plan and Measurement Plan.
- Collate Business Design Report. System Definition.
- Seek Project Board Approval.

12 TECHNICAL DESIGN STAGE

12.1 DEFINITION

Outline:

The Technical Design Stage follows acceptance of the Business Design Report by management, the System Definition by the User and authorization from the Project Board to proceed. During this Stage computer system design is carried out, to produce a computer solution In terms of program and file specifications.

Objectives:

- Specify all technical details of how the system will meet user requirements In terms of input, output. and processing,

- Produce an effective computer system design solution, and review the effect on hardware and software resources,

- Provide all necessary Information for use in the Development Stage, including program suite design and individual program specification and System Testing Plan,

- Review and revise Implementation and development plans,

- Produce a Design Specification for use In subsequent Stages,

- Issue a Design Report In order to obtain approval from User and DP Management,

- Update the System Definition If necessary.

12.2 TECHNICAL DESIGN STEPS

- **Technical Design Orientation**
- **Identify System Components**
- **Design Logical System**
- **Design Physical System**
- **Complete Detailed Design**
- **Plan System Testing**
- **Review Implementation And Development plans**
- **Draft And Review Design Documents**

12.3 SEEK APPROVAL.

Technical Design Stage Activities:

- **Review Systems Definition and Business Design Report to ensure understanding and completeness.**
- **Extract and identify Logical System components from activity documentation in the system Definition.**
- **Formulate Logical System components into a logical system design to present a full picture of the system.**
- **Produce a First Pass Physical Design (Programs, FILES/DB) from logical model. Size and refine until it meets the constraints of the system.**
- **Complete documentation of final Physical System.**

- Develop a detailed systems test plan. Identify test conditions, test data requirements, expected results and resources required.

- Update General Technical Plan and Macro Plan Produce next Stage Activity Plan and Measurement Plan.

- Collate Design Report. Design Specification.

- Seek Project Board Approval.

13 DEVELOPMENT STAGE

13.1 DEFINITION

Outline

The Development Stage follows acceptance of the Design Report by management and authorization from the Project Board to proceed. The Stage is concerned with converting the design defined in the Design Specification Into a complete working system including all necessary documentation and procedures.

The Stage can conveniently be subdivided into the following sub-Stages:

- Program Development
- Systems Testing
- Procedure Manual Production
- Installation Preparation.

Objectives:

- Design, code and test each program.
- test the system against the test plan agreed in the previous Stage
- develop all procedures and manuals necessary for the Implementation of the system,
- Prepare the Release Package for the next Stage.

- Review and revise implementation and development plans.

13.2 DEVELOPMENT STEPS

- Program Developmental
- Link Testing
- System Testing
- Procedure Manual Production
- Installation Preparation.

13.3 DEVELOPMENT STAGE ACTIVITIES

- Design, code and test each program.
- Link Test groups of programs identified on test plan.
- Carry out any further link testing between groups of programs and perform System Tests Identified on test plan. Carry out any amendments required to programs or documentation.
- Produce Operating Instructions, Data Control Instructions, Data Preparation Instruction and User Procedures.
- Ensure that all documentation in complete and produce the Release Package and Development Report. Update General Technical Plan and Macro Plan. Produce next Stage Activity; Plan and Measurement.

14 INSTALLATION STAGE

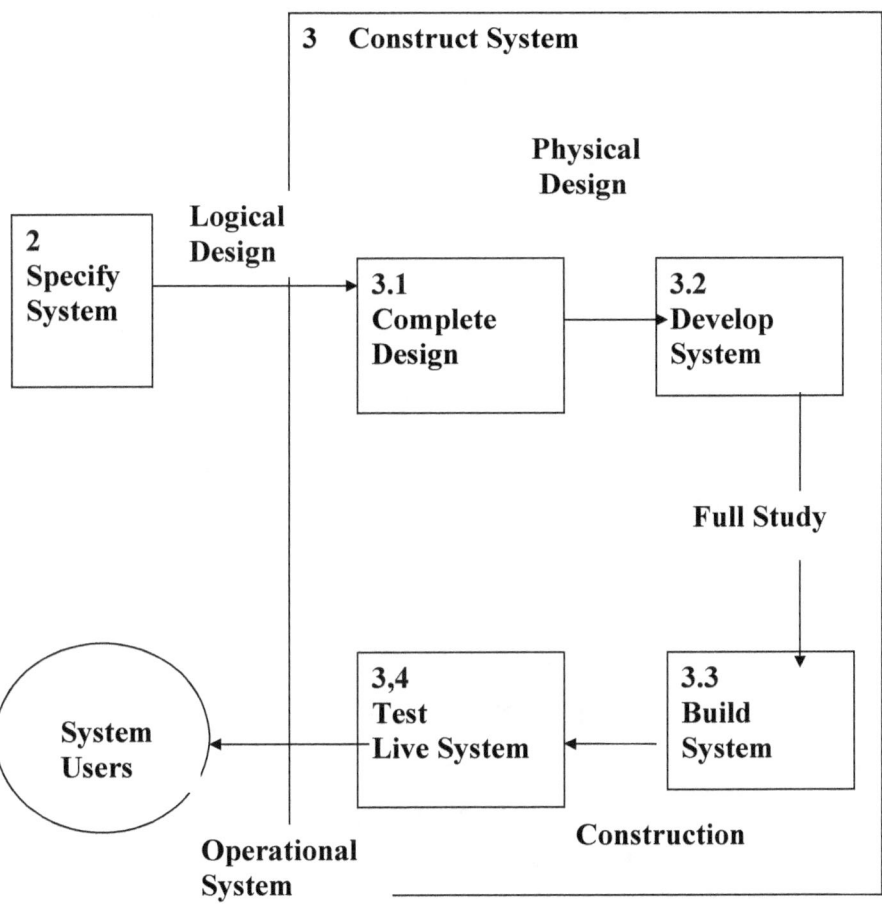

14.1 DEFINITION

Outline

This Stage follows production of the Release Package in the Development Stage, acceptance by management of the Development Report and authorization from the Project Board to proceed. The Stage is concerned with ensuring the acceptability of the system, both to the User and to Operations, and cut-over to live operation.

Objectives

- Ensure that the Release Package Is functioning correctly and to the satisfaction of the site development team,

- Carry out a series of tests to enable the User and Operations to formally accept the system,

- Cut-over to live operation.

14.2 INSTALLATION STEPS

- Installation Operation
- Install System
- Establish New Procedures
- Test System For Acceptance
- Complete Service Contract (Draft)
- Review Plans
- Seek Approval.

14.3 INSTALLATION STAGE ACTIVITIES

- Familiarize with and Review Release Package

- Set up and load test data
- Set up test libraries
- Set up on-line service
- Set up Security & Recovery
- Educate personnel
- Establish User liaison Procedures
- Establish Acceptance Testing Procedures
- Run Integrity Tests
- Run test environment
- Test Conversion software
- Draft Installation Report
- Seek Approval

15 OPERATIONS CONSOLIDATION STAGE

15.1 DEFINITION

Outline:

> The Operations Consolidation Stage is a recognition that following cut-over to the new System there will he a period during which the System is bedded in. The duration of this period will depend on the type and complexity of the System and the number of problems encountered. The main activities within the Stage are concerned with tuning the System, the procedures associated with it and the way it is being used. The Stage will continue until concluded by the Project Board but at least until the Post-Implementation Review has been conducted.

Objectives:

- Tune the System to optimize Its performance,
- Resolve immediate problems appearing In the System and log requests for changes,
- Install changes in the System to eliminate those off specifications or additional/changed requirements it has been agreed to implement,
- Refine and update all system documentation.

15.2 OPERATION CONSOLIDATION STEPS

- Operations Consolidation Orientation
- Cut Over To Production Running

- **Run Production System**
- **Finalize Service Contract (Draft)**
- **Review Report**
- **Seek Approval.**

15.3 OPERATION CONSOLIDATION ACTIVITIES

- **Review previous Stages**
- **Ensure everything required is available,**
- **Convert Files,**
- **Finalize Environment,**
- **Start System Operation,**
- **Bed in Application System,**
- **Tune Procedures,**
- **Identify additional and/or changed requirements,**
- **Prepare Operations Consolidation Report,**
- **Seek Approval to end Project.**

16 POST-IMPLEMENTATION REVIEW STAGE

16.1 DEFINITION

Outline

This is the last formal Stage in the Project development cycle, and will normally take place up to six months after the System goes live depending on the system cycle. The review team briefly examines the Operational System. When necessary a detailed examination of specific areas may be recommended and carried out. It is Important that resources to carry out the review ark, scheduled as part of the overall Project. The review will recommend whether the Project should be concluded or referred back to an earlier Stage. If the Project is referred back to an earlier Stage then this Stage must be re-entered and the appropriate reports updated prior to concluding the Project.

The Review is a specific activity providing a picture of the current position. And reviewing the history of the project to see what lessons may be learnt.

Objectives

- Review the performance of the computer system itself, against targets,
- Assess and categories requested changes,
- Review Operations procedures,
- Review Development techniques and procedures,

- Identify strengths and weaknesses, and decide whether or not an in-depth review of any area is necessary,

- Recommend any necessary changes,

- Review actual costs and benefits compared with original estimates,

16.3 POST-IMPLEMENTATION REVIEW STEPS

- Orientation And Planning

- Review System Operational

- Review User Procedures

- Review System Design

- Review Development Process

- Review Documentation

- Perform Cost And Benefits Analysis

- Produce Reports

- Seek Approval

- Close Down Project.

17 TECHNIQUES OVERVIEW

Typical Stages of Development

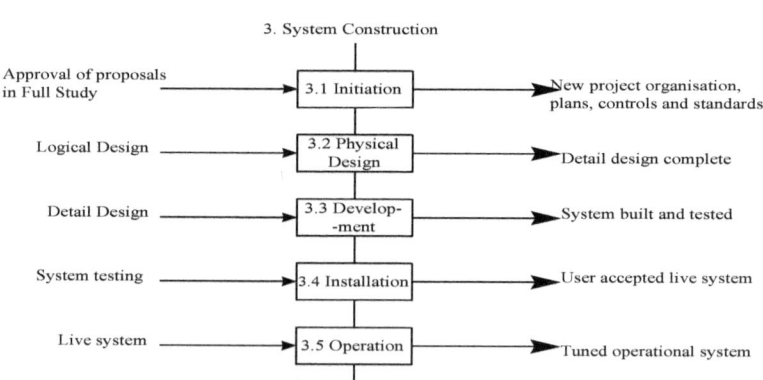

1. Feasibility Study

1.1 Initiation	→ Project organisation, plans, controls and standards
1.2 Problem Definition	
1.3 Project Identification	

2. Full Study

Approval of proposals in Feasibility Study → 2.1 Initiation → New project organisation plans, controls and standards

2.2 Specifica--tion → User specifications detailed

User Specifications → 2.3 Logical Design → Logical Design

3. System Construction

Approval of proposals in Full Study → 3.1 Initiation → New project organisation, plans, controls and standards

Logical Design → 3.2 Physical Design → Detail design complete

Detail Design → 3.3 Develop--ment → System built and tested

System testing → 3.4 Installation → User accepted live system

Live system → 3.5 Operation → Tuned operational system

17.1 ACCESS PROFILE

A diagrammatic representation of the access required to the DATA MODEL to achieve a particular function. Used In Specification Stages for checking technical viability of an option in the early stages.

17.2 ACTIVITY DIAGRAMS

A hierarchical diagramming method that shows the scope and activities in a system, the flow of information and storage of information. Well proven technique for conveying and testing understanding of a system. Used in Specification Stages.

17.3 ACTIVITY DOCUMENTATION

The documentation required to support activity diagrams i.e. Activity Descriptions, Data Flow Definitions. Data Store Definitions and Data Item Definitions. Used in Specification and Design Stages.

17.4 AUDIT CONSIDERATION

A set of techniques and a check list aimed at ensuring that the system produces correct results, works in accordance with laid down procedures, prevents fraud. Used in Specification and Technical Design Stages.

17.5 CODE READING

A formal examination of program code carried out by a programmer other than the programmer who wrote the program. Used in Development Stages.

17.6 DATA ANALYSIS

A set of techniques to break down the Information to be stored in a system; into its basic components, in order to understand the meaning of the Data and the relationships between the components. This is a well proven technique for conveying and testing understanding of system. Used in Specification and Technical Design Stages.

17.8 DATA GATHERING

A 'top down' method of gathering, questioning and sampling system data. Used in Specification Stages.

17.8 Data Structure Diagram

The pictorial representation of the structure of an input. Output or file. A technique known as Data Structure Enhancement is used during development to show a particular programs processing requirement. Used In Technical Design and Development Stages.

17.9 DESIGN REFINEMENT

A structured approach to the refinement of a systems design. Progresses from a direct Implementation of the logical design, to a practical physical design. The aim is to compromise the logical design as little as necessary and thus produce a design which is as maintainable as practicable. Used in Technical Design Stages.

17.10 FIRST PASS DATABASE DESIGN

The method of deriving a physical data base design from the data model produced during Business Design. The first pass design will model the business requirements as closely as the DBMS/ File handling facilities will allow. Used In Technical Design.

17.11 KEY PERFORMANCE FACTORS

A Key Performance Factor is an aspect of the business where good performance is vital. High level KPF's and their measures are input to Problem Analysis.

17.12 FIRST PASS PHYSICAL DESIGN

The purpose of first pass physical design is to translate the logical or unrestrained design of the system into a physical system which will run on the hardware and software provided. The first pass design may require refinement to meet performance requirements. Used in Technical Design Stages.

17.13 LANGUAGE CONVENTIONS

The conventions and styles applicable to particular languages (e.g. COBOL, FORTRAN) which enable people other than the original author to become familiar with a program. Based on the principle that source listing should form a major item of documentation. Used in Development Stages.

17.14 LOGICAL SYSTEMS CHART

A chart used to show processes and data in a batch system and their inter-relationships. The chart is produced by consideration of the business requirements but not performance/hardware constraints. Used in Technical Design Stages.

17.15 LOGICAL DESIGN CHART

A diagrammatic means of representing the entitles and their relationship in a data model. Used in Technical Design Stage.

17.16 MESSAGE STRUCTURE DIAGRAM

A diagrammatic technique for representing the structure of interactive transactions. Used in Technical Design Stages.

17.17 NORMALIZATION

The process of producing a Third Normal Form representation of the data in a system i.e. the most maintainable model of the entities to be stored, their keys, their attributes and the relationships between them. Used in Specification Stages.

17.18 PROBLEM ANALYSIS

The Techniques used to derive New User requirements by consideration of key performance factors and their associated measures. Used In Specifications Stage

17.19 PROCESS IDENTIFICATION

The methods used to identify the simplest units of processing which are to form the basis for physical programs. Used in Technical Design Stages.

17.20 PROGRAM LOGIC DESIGN

A set of techniques for producing a logical program design. Used in Development Stages.

17.21 PROGRAM OPTIMIZATION

A set of techniques which may be used (if necessary) to improve program performance. The aim is to achieve the greatest benefit with the minimum of damage to the logical design. Used in Development Stages.

17.22 PROGRAM TEST PLANNING

Technique to produce a set of test data which will adequately test the program. The degree of testing will depend on the reliability required of the program. Used in Development Stages.

17.23 SIZING

The techniques used to estimate at design time whether or not a system can meet its design objectives. Used in Technical Design Stages.

17.24 STRUCTURED ENGLISH

Used for describing processes rules of activity diagrams. Uses standard format, style and logic constraint suitable for describing procedure. Used in Specification Stages.

17.25 STRUCTURED WALKTHROUGHS

Form of a meeting designed to encourage error detection, spread familiarly within projects. Harmony as style and method. Used in All Stages.

17.26 SYSTEMS TEST PLANNING

A set of techniques designed to identify the systems test considerations, test cases, expected results etc. and to plan the carrying out of such tests. Used in Technical Design and Development Stages.

18 DOCUMENTATION

18.1 BUSINESS DESIGN REPORT

Purpose:

To report to User and DP Management on the conduct of the Business Design Stage and to provide sufficient Information to enable the justification for the project to be re-assessed prior to the Technical Design Stage.

Contents:

Introduction, Management Summary, Requirements Summary, Proposed System, Implications of the proposed system, Future Requirements,

Plus Appendices for Installation Strategy, Education Strategy, Computer Resource Requirements, Costs and Benefits.

18.2 DESIGN SPECIFICATION

Purpose:

To provide documentation of the designed system for use during the Program Development, Testing and Implementation. The design Specification also indexes all Programs, Files and Data Bases used by the system.

Contents:

Introduction, Files and Databases Summary, Programs Summary, Security and Controls, Interfaces with System Software. Plus appendices for Physical Design Chart, Message Structure Diagrams, Sizing Charts, Design Decisions.

18.3 DEVELOPMENT REPORT

Purpose:

The Development Report provides an opportunity for Management to make an assessment of the progress of the project and to decide whether the project should proceed Into the Installation Stage.

Contents:

Introduction, Management Summary, Release Package. Plus Appendices for Installation Strategy, Educational Strategy. Computer Resource Requirements Costs and Benefits, User Acceptance Strategy, Operations Acceptance Criteria.

18.4 EXISTING SYSTEM

Purpose:

To provide sufficient understanding of the requirements of a system to enable good judgments to be made for the objectives of the new system.

Contents:

As for Systems Definition, in principle, but not necessarily in same form or to same level of detail.

18.5 INSTALLATION REPORT

Purpose:

To report on the findings of the Installation Stage, Update the findings of the Development Report, Define the actions for the next Stage.

Contents:

Introduction, Management Summary, Operational System Description. Operations Acceptance Agreement, User Acceptance Agreement. Plus Appendices for Computer

Resources Requirements, Cost and Benefits, Off-Specifications, Additional/changed requirements.

18.6 JUSTIFICATION REPORT

Purpose:

To assess the technical and financial feasibility of a proposed system. This provides the Users and DP Management with sufficient information to decide whether and on what basis, the project should continue to the Requirement Definition Stage.

Contents:

Introduction. Management Summary, Existing System, Requirements Summary, Options Considered, Implications of proposed system, Future Requirements. Plus Appendices for Installation Strategy, Education Strategy, Computer Resources Requirement. Cost and Benefits.

18.7 OPERATIONAL SYSTEMS

Purpose:

A record of the history of System variants and their component System Deliverables for quality assurance.

Contents:

System Deliverable History and System variant Definition.

18.8 RELEASE PACKAGE

Purpose:

To provide the Installation Stage team with all the components of the system and the details of the medium on which it is delivered which will enable them to set up and run the System.

Contents:

Software - load module, subroutine, Specification, Database Definition, Screen Format, TP Monitor, Table Entry.

Test Data - Installation Test, Acceptance Test. Documentation - System Definition, Design Specifications, Development Report, Installation, User and Operations Manuals.

18.9 SYSTEMS DEFINITION

Purpose:

To provide primary documentation of the system for the User. Provide documentation of the system for Technical Design.

Contents:

Introduction, Business Requirements, System Description, Computer Facilities. Plus Appendices for Data Model, Access Profiles, Dataflow Definitions.

18.10 TECHNICAL DESIGN REPORT

Purpose:

To report to User and DP Management on the conduct of the Technical Design Stage and to provide sufficient Information to enable the justification for,-the project to be re-assessed prior to the Development Stage.

Contents:

Introduction, Management Summary, System Requirements Summary. Security and Controls summary, Performance Requirements Summary, System Description. Plus Appendices for Installation Strategy, Education Strategy, Computer Resource Requirements, Cost and Benefits, User Acceptance Strategy, Operations Acceptance Strategy, Systems Test Plan.

18.11 Terms of Reference

Purpose:

To define the scope of the Justification Stage of a Project i.e. for the enhancement/re-development of a System.

Contents:

Task Definition. Constraints, Expected Benefits, Plus Appendix for reference documents.

18.12 User Requirement Report

Purpose:

Report on the findings of the User Requirement Definition Stage; Update the findings of the Justification Report, Define Actions for Business Design.

Contents:

Introduction, Management Summary, Requirements Summary, Options Considered, Implication of Proposed System, Future Requirements. Plus Appendices for Installation strategy. Education Strategy, Computer

Resource Requirements. Cost and Benefits, Other items specific to particular projects.

18.13 USER REQUIREMENT SPECIFICATION

Purpose:

To define the User Requirement in detail and to outline a system which will meet the Requirement?

Contents:

Introduction, Business Requirement. System outline, Computer Facilities. Plus Appendices for Major Data flow definitions.

Typical Stages of Development

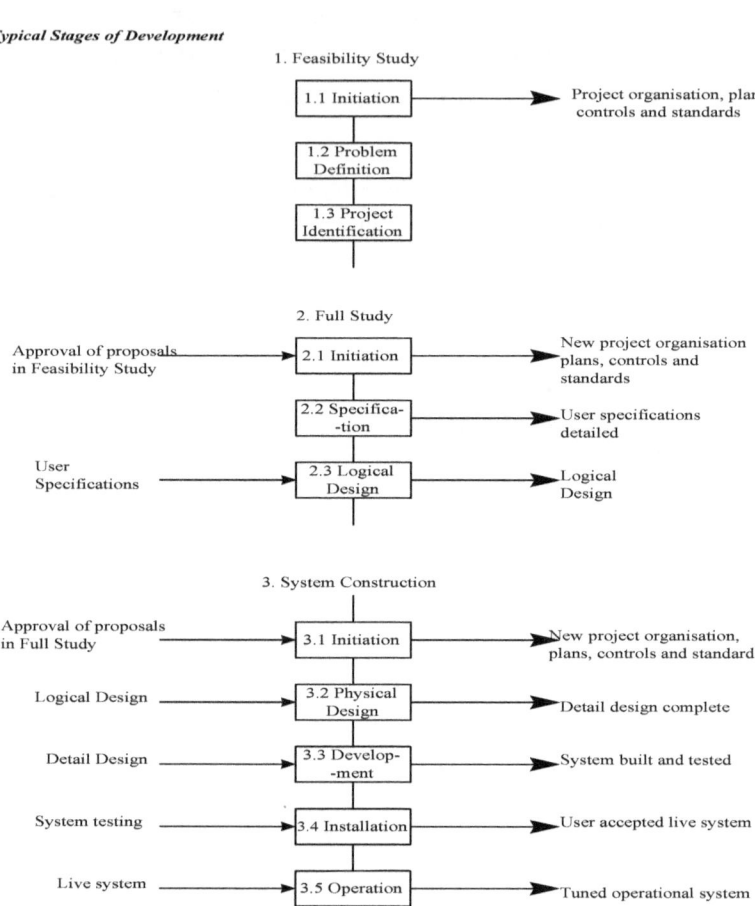

Typical stage flow through an IT development life cycle. The number of stages, their names and the point at which each one ends are determined by the needs of the project.

19 BENEFITS

The benefits of the 'DEFINE THAT SYSTEM' procedures can be summarized as follows.

1. Provides the basis for controlling the implementation of strategic business plans.

2. Promotes the business view for the justification of projects and provides mechanisms for ensuring their ongoing viability and business integrity.

3. The organization structure encourages user and business participation at all levels and can be tailored to any type, size and complexity of project.

4. Separates and clearly identifies and defines the roles and responsibilities in project management.

5. The stage concept provides the basis for conscious and continuous management control.

6. Concentrates on the real goals of the project, through the products, to ensure a common understanding about what is being produced. This product orientation also enables better estimating, planning and control.

7. The planning and control mechanisms are tailored and structured to one another.

8. Quality is planned, controlled and assured from the outset of the project.

9. Provides an excellent vehicle for encouraging the right people to make the right decision at the right time.

10. Confronts the management of risk and uncertainty by asking questions and forcing issues into the open. Project costs can be reduced by dealing with issues before they become problems. Simplifies paperwork, by concentrating on essential documentation and the provision of simple but effective reporting procedures.

The main benefits, as listed above, have been attributed by actual users.

END

INDEX:

BIBLIOGRAPHY:
(ALL BOOKS LISTED BELOW ARE WRITTEN BY ANDREAS SOFRONIOU)

1. I.T. RISK MANAGEMENT, ISBN: 978-1-4467-5653-9
2. SYSTEMS ENGINEERING, ISBN: 978-1-4477-7553-9
3. BUSINESS INFORMATION SYSTEMS, CONCEPTS AND EXAMPLES, ISBN: 978-1-4092-7338-7 & 0952795639
4. A GUIDE TO INFORMATION TECHNOLOGY, ISBN: 978-1-4092-7608-1 & 0952795647
5. CHANGE MANAGEMENT, ISBN: 978-1-4457-6114-5
6. CHANGE MANAGEMENT IN I.T., ISBN: 978-1-4092-7712-5 & 0952725355
7. CHANGE MANAGEMENT IN SYSTEMS, ISBN: 978-1-4457-1099-0
8. FRONT-END DESIGN AND DEVELOPMENT FOR SYSTEMS APPLICATIONS ISBN: 978-1-4092-7588-6 & 0952725347
9. I.T RISK MANAGEMENT ISBN: 978-1-4092-7488-9 & 0952725320
10. THE SIMPLIFIED PROCEDURES FOR I.T. PROJECTS DEVELOPMENT, ISBN: 978-1-4092-7562-6 & 0952725312
11. THE SIGMA METHODOLOGY FOR RISK MANAGEMENT IN SYSTEMS DEVELOPMENT, ISBN: 978-1-4092-7690-6 & 095279568X
12. TRADING ON THE INTERNET IN THE YEAR 2000 AND BEYOND, ISBN: 978-1-4092- 7577 & 0952795671
13. STRUCTURED SYSTEMS METHODOLOGY ISBN: 978-1-4477-6610-0

14. SYSTEMS MANAGEMENT, ISBN: 978-1-4710-4907-1, 978-1-4710-4891-3, 978-1-4710-4903-3
15. INFORMATION TECHNOLOGY LOGICAL ANALYSIS, ISBN: 978-1-4717-1688-1
16. I.T. RISKS LOGICAL ANALYSIS, ISBN: 978-1-4717-1957-8
17. I.T. CHANGES LOGICAL ANALYSIS, ISBN: 978-1-4717-2288-2
18. LOGICAL ANALYSIS OF SYSTEMS, RISKS, CHANGES, ISBN: 978-1-4717-2294-3
19. MANAGE THAT I.T. PROJECT, ISBN: 978-1-4717-5304-6
20. COMPUTING, A PRÉCIS ON SYSTEMS, SOFTWARE AND HARDWARE, ISBN: 978-1-2910-5102-5
21. MANAGEMENT OF I.T. CHANGES, RISKS, WORKSHOPS, EPISTEMOLOGY, ISBN: 978-1-84753-147-6
22. THE MANAGEMENT OF COMMERCIAL COMPUTING, ISBN: 978-1-4092-7550-3 & 0952795604
23. PROGRAMME MANAGEMENT WORKSHOP, ISBN: 978-1-4092-7583-1& 0952725371
24. THE PHILOSOPHICAL CONCEPTS OF MANAGEMENT THROUGH THE AGES, ISBN: 978-1-4092-7554-1 & 0952725363
25. The Management Of Projects, Systems, Internet, And Risks, ISBN: 978-1-4092-7464-3 & 0952795698